LET'S PLAY
Martial Arts

Karen Durrie

www.av2books.com

AV² provides enriched content that supplements and complements this book. Weigl's AV² books strive to create inspired learning and engage young minds in a total learning experience.

Your AV² Media Enhanced books come alive with...

Audio
Listen to sections of the book read aloud.

Video
Watch informative video clips.

Embedded Weblinks
Gain additional information for research.

Try This!
Complete activities and hands-on experiments.

Key Words
Study vocabulary, and complete a matching word activity.

Quizzes
Test your knowledge.

Slide Show
View images and captions, and prepare a presentation.

... and much, much more!

Go to **www.av2books.com**, and enter this book's unique code.

BOOK CODE

W458052

AV² by Weigl brings you media enhanced books that support active learning.

Published by AV² by Weigl
350 5th Avenue, 59th Floor New York, NY 10118
Website: www.av2books.com   www.weigl.com

Durrie, Karen.
 Martial arts / Karen Durrie.
    p. cm. -- (Let's play)
 ISBN 978-1-61690-941-3 (hardcover : alk. paper) -- ISBN 978-1-61690-587-3 (online)
 1. Martial arts--Juvenile literature. I. Title.
 GV1101.35.D87 2011
 796.815--dc23
                          2011023433

Printed in the United States of America in North Mankato, Minnesota
1 2 3 4 5 6 7 8 9 0 15 14 13 12 11

062011
WEP030611

Project Coordinator: Karen Durrie Art Director: Terry Paulhus

Weigl acknowledges Getty Images as the primary image supplier for this title.

LET'S PLAY Martial Arts

CONTENTS

I love martial arts.
I am going
to martial arts today.

4

Like a PRO

Martial arts began thousands of years ago.

5

I get dressed
for martial arts.
I put on a white suit.
I tie my yellow belt.

A martial arts suit is called a Gi.

7

I go to my class.
I see my friends.

Like a PRO

We stretch first to warm up our muscles.

I bow to the teacher. The teacher shows us what to do.

Kung fu and karate are two kinds of martial arts.

I need strong legs and arms.
I need to watch and listen.

The more I do martial arts the better I get.

I kick with my feet.
I punch with my hands.
We all do the same moves.

Like a PRO

We do
martial arts
in bare feet.

15

Kicking and punching make me thirsty.

Like a PRO

Water keeps
me healthy.
I have a drink.

17

I do martial arts
with my friend.
I flip him over.

Many classes have padded floors.

I get a new belt.
It is orange.
I am happy.
I love martial arts.

MARTIAL ARTS FACTS

This page provides more detail about the interesting facts found in the book.
Simply look at the corresponding page number to match the fact.

Pages 4-5

Martial arts are a form of self-defense and are not to be used for aggression or violence. Most types teach people to protect themselves using their hands, arms, feet, legs, and body. Many martial arts practiced today have their roots in ancient Asia, but forms of martial arts were also done in other parts of the world.

Pages 6–7

The Gi consists of a jacket tied with a belt and short pants. The loose fit allows for comfort and ease of movement. The fabric is very durable to withstand the pulling and contact of martial arts. The Gi can come in many colors but is most commonly seen in white or black.

Pages 8–9

Cold muscles are stiff, and sudden twisting and turning can cause injury. Warming and stretching muscles before martial arts can reduce the risk of injury. Warm muscles are more flexible and produce energy faster for the quick moves of martial arts.

Pages 10–11

Bowing to a teacher—who is usually called a sensei—is a sign of respect. Bowing is done in most martial arts. There are hundreds of types of martial arts. Some copy the movements of animals, while others use bamboo swords or sticks. Judo, Tae Kwan Do, and Tai Chi are some other types of martial arts.

Pages 12–13

The mind and the body get exercise with martial arts. Focus, discipline, patience, and self-control are all things that people may learn from martial arts. Taking part can also help children build confidence and self-esteem. For the body, martial arts help develop increased balance, strength, and flexibility.

Pages 14–15

A typical martial arts class involves a warm-up, basic stances, and moves. Moves include punches, kicks, blocks, and strikes, moving on the spot, or across the floor. Sequences of moves are also taught. Students will often practice the same moves and sequences in unison.

Pages 16–17

If you are exercising or playing sports, your body needs more water than usual. If your body does not have enough water, you will not be as fast or sharp as you would like to be. Water is important for helping your body stay at a healthy temperature.

Pages 18–19

Students may learn to use their strength and moves to defeat an opponent in a martial arts match. Different types of martial arts involve wearing protective gear. Students are taught how to fall to reduce the potential for injury. There are rules for competitions that include places on the body you cannot strike a competitor.

Pages 20–21

Skill levels in martial arts are rated by different colored belts. White is the first belt, and in many types of martial arts, black is the expert belt, with many colors of belts in between. Students must pass a skill test given by their sensei to get the next color belt. It can take people a very long time to earn a black belt.

WORD LIST

Research has shown that as much as 65 percent of all written material published in English is made up of 300 words. These 300 words cannot be taught using pictures or learned by sounding them out. They must be recognized by sight. This book contains 47 common sight words to help young readers improve their reading fluency and comprehension. This book also teaches young readers several important content words. These words are paired with pictures to aid in learning and improve understanding.

Page	Sight Words First Appearance	Page	Content Words First Appearance
4	I, to	4	arts, martial, today
5	began, of, years	6	belt, suit
6	a, for, get, my, on, put, white	7	Gi
7	is	8	class, friends
8	go, see	9	muscles
9	first, our, up, we	10	teacher
10	do, shows, the, what	11	karate, kung fu
11	and, are, kinds, two	12	arms, legs
12	need, watch	17	drink
13	more	18	friend
14	all, feet, hands, moves, same, with	19	floors
15	in		
16	make, me		
17	have, keeps, water		
18	him, over		
19	many		
20	it, new		

Animal Habitats

The Frog in the Pond

Text by Jennifer Coldrey

Photographs by
Oxford Scientific Films

Gareth Stevens Children's Books
MILWAUKEE

Frogs and where they live

Frogs are *amphibians*. This means that they can live both on land and in water. First as eggs, and then as tadpoles, they start their life in freshwater ponds and pools, later coming out onto land as adult frogs. But although the adults can live on land, they have to return to water to lay their eggs.

Frogs can be found both in and around ponds in many parts of the world. They never move very far away from water and can only survive on land in damp, shady places. This is because a frog has a very thin skin which is not waterproof and which has to be kept moist; otherwise the body loses water and the frog dries up and dies. Frogs also breathe partly through their skin, which needs to be kept moist so that oxygen can pass in easily.

Unlike adult frogs, tadpoles can only survive in water. The pond they live in is their whole world, and here they must find food and shelter. There is usually plenty to eat in a pond — lots of plants, as well as many insects and other tiny animals. Unfortunately, there are also lots of hungry animals that like to eat tadpoles. The tadpoles can protect themselves to some extent by hiding among water weeds or under stones, but many are killed and eaten by *predators*. Adult frogs have enemies in a pond too, but they are better protected than tadpoles because of their larger size and wonderful *camouflage*. They can also escape by hopping away to safety on land.

The European Common Frog is hard to see as it sits in the shallows among the mud and water plants.

These dark wriggling tadpoles show up clearly in this shallow pool.

A pond can be a dangerous place to live. It is a small *habitat* which can change dramatically under certain conditions. In bitterly cold weather the water may freeze, while in a hot, dry summer, many ponds dry up completely. Sometimes the amount of oxygen in the water can drop to very low levels, making it difficult for pond animals to breathe. Ponds can also become overgrown with reeds and other tall plants, which gradually creep in from the edges and silt up the ground, until there is no water left.

For tadpoles there is no way of escaping if things go wrong. But frogs can survive many of these disasters by burrowing down into the mud or by moving to a safe place of shelter on land.

This peaceful pond is an ideal place for frogs to live.

3

A Red-eyed Tree Frog from the tropical forests of Panama.

A tiny tree frog shelters in a cup of rainwater, caught between the leaves of a bromeliad plant.

How frogs survive around the world

Frogs cannot survive in extremely hot or extremely cold places. They are cold-blooded animals, which means that their body temperature changes according to their surroundings. In hot weather their bodies get warmer, while in cold weather their body temperature goes down. (Warm-blooded animals, such as birds and mammals, have a fairly warm body temperature which always stays the same, in spite of the weather.)

Frogs can easily die of cold so, in places like England and North America, when winter comes, they hide away under stones or in holes in the ground, or they burrow deep into the mud of ponds and ditches. Here they go into a long, deep sleep called *hibernation* and do not wake up until warmer weather returns.

In tropical countries it never gets very cold, so frogs do not need to hibernate. Here, many frogs live up in the trees or on the forest floor among the cool, damp leaves. Because the atmosphere in the jungle is so moist, these frogs can survive quite happily out of water for much of the time. But many still lay their eggs in pools or puddles. Sometimes the nursery pool is nothing more than a tiny cup of rainwater caught between the leaves of plants or in a tree hollow. And, in some cases, the tadpoles grow into frogs without being in a pool at all!

In hot, dry places like Australia, Africa, and parts of North America, there are even some frogs that can live in the desert. These frogs spend most of their lives asleep in burrows underground. Only when it rains do they wake up and struggle to the surface. They lay their eggs in the shallow pools that form on the desert floor, and the tadpoles hatch and grow into tiny frogs in only a few weeks. This gives them just enough time to develop before the pools dry up and disappear. When the short rainy season comes to an end, the frogs absorb a lot of water and their bodies swell. Their skin produces a thick, slimy coat which covers the body like a plastic bag, and this prevents them from drying out during their long time underground.

An Australian burrowing frog digs its way out of the sand as the rain soaks down into the ground.

A bullfrog resting on a log. These frogs can grow to 8 inches (20cm) long.

The frog's body

Most frogs have a bullet-shaped body, with a broad, pointed head and a very wide mouth. They have a smooth, moist skin which feels slimy and often rather cool. Frogs have lungs for breathing on land, but they also take in some oxygen through their skin. When underwater they breathe through their skin much more, but they also have to come to the surface occasionally to fill their lungs with air. Frogs can absorb water through their skin, so they do not need to drink.

Many tropical frogs are brightly colored, but the skin of most common frogs is a yellowish- or greenish-brown, marked with various spots and streaks of black, brown, or red. This mottled patterning is useful for camouflage, both on land and in water, as it helps to break up the frog's outline against its background.

The spotted skin of the Leopard Frog blends in with its background and disguises it well.

Frogs can slowly change the color of their skins to match their surroundings. They can do this because of special dark cells scattered throughout the skin, which can either shrink or spread out, making the body look either paler (and yellowish-green) or darker (and brownish). The patterned markings never change.

However, it is often the shadow of an animal which makes it stand out against the ground. Many frogs are pale underneath, and this helps to camouflage them on land by lessening their shadow. The light belly is also useful underwater, because hungry fishes, swimming below, cannot see the frog's pale body against the light when they look up through the water.

A frog's skin is very sensitive to touch and to changes in its surroundings, such as the temperature of the water in a pond, or the amount of moisture in the air. These changes can also affect the color of the skin.

Frogs shed their skin several times a year. The outer layer splits and peels, and the frog uses its feet to pull it off, usually eating the old skin afterwards. A brighter, soft new skin now covers its body.

Female frogs are usually larger than males. But this is not so with some of the bullfrogs, where the male may be two or three times bigger than the female.

A hungry fish, looking up from below, would not see the pale shape of this frog hiding beneath a water-lily leaf.

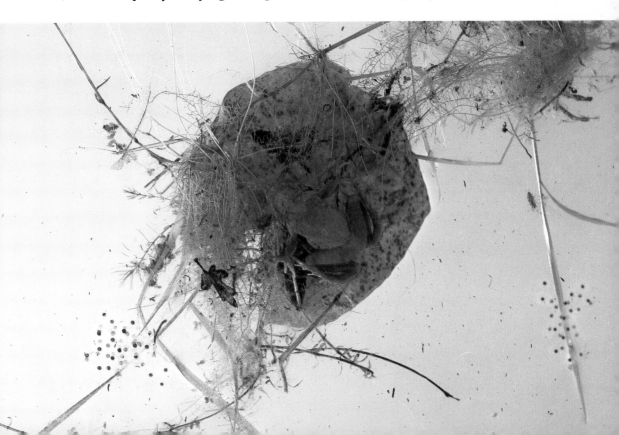

The head of a green tree frog from Australia.

The frog's head

A frog's large bulging eyes stick out prominently from the top of its head. This gives it a good all-round view of its surroundings, without having to turn its head. The thick eyelids never close, but each lower lid has a special thin *membrane*, like an inner eyelid, which can move quickly across the eye to clean off any dirt. These membranes cover and protect the eyes underwater. In some frogs they are transparent, but in others they are patterned with many beautiful stripes and markings which can be useful for camouflage when they are drawn across the shining eyes to hide them from predators.

At the front of the head are two small nostrils which open into the roof of the mouth. These are used for breathing as well as for smelling. As a frog breathes air in and out of its nostrils, you can see its throat moving up and down continually as it swallows the air down into its lungs. When underwater, frogs keep their nostrils closed.

All we can see of a frog's ears are two small round patches of thin skin, one on each side of the head just behind the eyes. These are the eardrums, which cover the opening to the ears. Frogs can hear quite well, and they communicate with each other by singing and croaking, especially in the breeding season.

This male tree frog puffs out a huge air bubble under his chin as he sings noisily in the night.

Male frogs sing or croak by pumping air backwards and forwards over their vocal cords at the back of the throat. When doing this, they keep their mouth and nostrils firmly closed. Frogs like the European Common Frog increase the sound by puffing out their throats to form a pouch. Other frogs have a flap of very loose skin on their throats which they puff out into a huge bubble to make the sound more resonant. Some frogs produce two bubbles of air, one on each side of the head. Each kind of frog has its own special call, varying from small peeps and trills to the deep booming of the bullfrogs. Female frogs make noises too, but they never sing or croak, and only produce an occasional grunt during the breeding season.

A male Edible Frog calls to attract females to the pond. He has two air bubbles one on either side of his throat.

9

Tree frogs, like this one from Trinidad, are expert climbers and leapers. Each toe ends in a suction pad.

Legs and movement

Frogs are flattish and streamlined in shape, with legs that are well adapted for movement both on land and in water. Their front legs are short and stumpy, with four toes on each foot. Sometimes frogs use their front feet to help stuff food into their mouths. The back legs are extremely long, with very powerful muscles; they are useful for swimming as well as for leaping. Some frogs can jump enormous distances on land — up to eight or nine times their own length in one leap! One of the best jumpers is the Leopard Frog, which can leap up to 13 times its own length, while one of the large African bullfrogs has been known to jump a distance of 14 feet. The frog's back feet have five long toes which are webbed. These act like paddles underwater and help the frog to swim well.

Tree frogs are even more specialized for the life they lead. They are agile climbers, with feet adapted for clinging onto reeds, branches, and tree-trunks. They have small ridges on the soles of their feet which help them to grip, and each toe ends in a flat, round suction pad which can cling tightly to smooth, upright, or even overhanging surfaces.

Right: A Leopard Frog uses his powerful back legs to leap up out of the water.

A frog cleans the dirt off an earthworm with its front feet, before eating it.

Food and feeding

Adult frogs feed mainly on insects, but they also eat worms, slugs, snails, and spiders. Their good eyesight helps them to spot their *prey*. As soon as they see a small creature moving, they strike out at it with their tongues. A frog's tongue is long and sticky. It is attached to the front end of the mouth and flicks out like a strip of fly-paper to catch food. If the prey is good to eat, the frog takes it into its large mouth and swallows it. Although it has no real teeth, a frog has many tiny, tooth-like fangs around the edges of its jaws, which help it to grip slippery prey. When it swallows, its large eyeballs press down onto the roof of its mouth and this helps to push the food down its throat. When this happens the frog looks as though it is blinking.

The frog finally gulps down the worm by "blinking" its eyes. This helps to push the food down its throat.

A frog's long tongue is joined to the front of its mouth. It can flick it out quickly to catch moving prey.

Frogs have good enough eyesight to be able to leap out of the water to catch flying insects such as butterflies, gnats, and flies. They will strike at almost anything that moves, and this can be painful if the prey turns out to be a bee or a wasp! Most frogs catch their food on land, but some (like the Marsh Frog and Edible Frog) which spend a lot of their time in water, feed on small pond animals such as shrimps, worms, insect *larvae*, and tiny fishes, which they catch underwater. Some of the large bullfrogs eat quite big prey, including baby water birds, young turtles, and some small fishes. They also eat smaller frogs and tadpoles, including their own brothers and sisters! This is quite common in other frogs too, and many turn *cannibal* if food becomes scarce.

Sometimes large frogs eat smaller frogs.

During mating, the male frog clasps the female tightly with his strong front legs.

Mating and breeding

Most frogs lay their eggs in water and many breed in much the same way as the Common European Frog. The breeding season begins in early spring, when the weather is just starting to get warmer. The frogs come out of hibernation and make their way to a pond to mate. They usually return to the pond where they were born and may travel several miles to get there, although many hibernate close by. The males arrive first, croaking and calling to attract the females.

In the breeding season, male frogs develop a thick, black, horny pad on each thumb. This helps them to grasp the female's fat, slippery body.

Frogs usually gather in large groups at a breeding pool, and the sounds of their chorus can sometimes be heard for up to half a mile away. The calling of the first arrivals probably helps to guide others to the pool, although many frogs seem to find their way by smell, or by recognizing landmarks on the way. Many travel by night when they may be guided by the stars. Mating takes place at night and there is no courtship beforehand. Each male simply grabs the nearest female and climbs onto her back. He clasps her tightly under the arms with his strong front legs. The females are now very fat because their bodies are full of eggs.

The mating pairs stay clasped together for several hours, or sometimes for several days. At last, the female lays her eggs. She squeezes them out of her body, by pressing down with her front legs. In only a few seconds she produces a mass of several thousand eggs. At the same time, the male sheds a cloud of *sperm* over the eggs to fertilize them. The female then gives a little grunt and the male lets go of her. The two frogs separate and the female hops away, but males usually stay at the pond to look for other females to mate with. If there are very few females around, the males often fight over them and sometimes a female is drowned when several males climb on top of her.

The male and female separate soon after the eggs have been laid.

Newly-laid frogspawn of the European Common Frog.

Eggs and tadpoles

Frogs usually lay their eggs in shallow water. Some leave them to float on the surface, while others attach them to stones or water plants in the pond. Most females produce several hundreds, if not thousands, of eggs. Other frogs lay fewer, either leaving them in several small clumps, or, as with the European Common Frog, in one large mass.

Nearly everyone knows what frogspawn looks like. Each round, black egg is surrounded by a thick layer of jelly, and the eggs stick together in a mass, making it very difficult for predators to eat them. The jelly is slippery and unpleasant to taste; it also protects the eggs from the cold.

The eggs of the European Common Frog first sink to the bottom of the pond, but then the jelly gradually swells, and the mass of spawn floats up to the surface. Here the eggs are warmed in the sun.

They start to grow and change their shape and, after about two weeks, tiny black tadpoles hatch out. The tadpoles wriggle free of the jelly, but they stay nearby, clinging to weeds or other frogspawn by special suckers on their heads. During the next few days they live on the remains of the egg yolk inside their bodies. But their mouths soon develop. They then start to feed on water plants, using their tough, horny lips to nibble and bite.

When they hatch out, the tiny black tadpoles cling to the jelly with their sucker mouths.

Tadpoles breathe underwater through their *gills*, which absorb oxygen from the water directly into the blood stream. A tadpole's first gills are feathery-looking branches which stick out into the water just behind the head. These later become covered with skin, and a new set of gills starts to form in a gill chamber inside the body. Water is pumped into the gill chamber through the mouth and then out through a small hole on the left side of the body. Fishes breathe in much the same way.

At first the young tadpoles only wriggle, but as they get bigger they start to swim about actively. Their long tails and streamlined shape help them to move easily through the water.

A young tadpole breathes through its gills, which stick out as tufts, one on each side of the body.

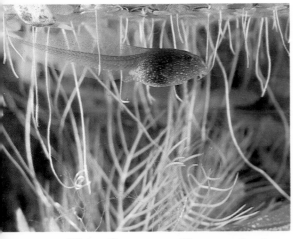

This Common Frog tadpole now has gills inside its body. It nibbles at the water weeds with its horny lips.

By 5-6 weeks, the back legs are growing.

From tadpole to frog

As the tadpoles grow bigger, their diet changes and they start to eat tiny pond animals, as well as dead animal flesh and even other tadpoles. They become *omnivorous*, and this extra protein from meat enables them to develop properly into frogs.

Later, the front legs start to push through.

At 12 weeks, the tadpole now has four legs.

As the tail gets shorter, the young froglet comes to the surface to breathe air.

These young frogs, now ½-¾" (12-15mm) long, have hopped out of the pond onto land.

At about five weeks, two small stumps appear at the base of the tail. These are the back legs, which, after another two or three weeks, have grown into jointed legs with toes. By eight or nine weeks, the tadpole has grown lungs inside its body to replace the gills. It now needs to come to the surface to gulp air. At ten weeks, the front legs are starting to push through at the front of the body and the tail has begun to shorten.

During the next few weeks, the legs grow to full size and the tail becomes shorter and shorter. At between three and four months, the young froglets are ready to come out on land. They hop away into the damp grass or sit about on rocks in the water, ready to jump to safety if danger threatens.

Sometimes, if there is not enough food or the weather is very cold, tadpoles take much longer to grow into frogs. Some may even spend the winter in hibernation before continuing their development. On the other hand, the tadpoles of frogs living in hot, dry countries develop very quickly and may grow into adult frogs in only a week or two.

Most young frogs continue to grow for two or three years. They become fully grown and are themselves able to breed at three years, or at five years in the case of some bullfrogs.

A pair of African tree frogs with their nest of foam.

Some unusual ways of breeding

Not all frogs lay their eggs in water. Some leave them in wet, mossy ground, while others dig small nesting burrows into damp soil or mud, where they lay their eggs. In some cases, the tadpoles hatch out and then slither down into a nearby pool when it rains; but, in others, these nesting places are damp enough for the tadpoles to stay and develop into frogs without the need for a pool.

Some African tree frogs make a special nest of foam for their eggs. They mate on leaves or branches overhanging a pool and, when the eggs are laid, the frogs cover them with a lot of sticky, clear liquid. Both parents use their back legs to whip up this syrupy "egg-white" into a frothy mass of foam. This hardens like a meringue around the hundred or so newly-laid eggs. It is moist inside the foam nest, and here the young tadpoles hatch out in safety, well protected from their enemies and from the heat of the sun. The female frog stays to guard the nest and, after a week or so, the foam dissolves away underneath and the tadpoles drop into the water below.

The male South American glass frog sits close to its eggs for the first day or two to keep them moist.

Some tropical frogs lay their eggs on moist leaves and stay nearby to guard them. After hatching, the tadpoles drop into a pool below where they continue to grow. But in some tree frogs, the egg-jelly turns to liquid and forms a tiny, watery pool, in which each tadpole develops while still on its leaf. Other frogs carry their eggs and young around with them on their bodies, on their backs, or under a flap of skin, or sometimes in their mouths or in a special brood pouch. In many cases, the tadpoles are eventually taken to a pool and set free in the water; but, in the case of some strange frogs, the tadpoles are tended by the parent until they grow into tiny froglets.

Looking after eggs and young is rather unusual in the frog world, since most common frogs leave their eggs to grow and develop on their own.

The eggs of this small frog develop into tadpoles under a pouch of skin on the mother's back.

Hedgehogs sometimes catch and eat frogs.

Frogs and their enemies

Frogs are hunted and eaten by many animals both on land and in the water. Their enemies on land include snakes, rats, foxes, hedgehogs, badgers, stoats, weasels, and crows, as well as many birds of prey such as owls and hawks.

They are not safe in a large pond either, since birds such as herons and gulls may come down to grab them, while turtles, otters, and snakes may catch them in the water. Under the water, large fish, like pike and perch, stalk them from below.

A heron peers into the water and waits to stab a passing frog or fish.

Fortunately, frogs have many different ways of escaping from their enemies. Their skin usually blends in well with their surroundings, so, providing they keep still, predators often do not see them. When resting in a pond, they often sit quietly in the shallows, with only their eyes, ears and nostrils peeping above the surface to keep a look-out for danger.

If a shadow passes over them or they become alarmed in any way, they usually hop away to a safe hiding place. Most frogs leap to safety when alarmed. Sometimes they jump into the water with a loud splash, causing ripples on the surface, which makes it difficult for a land animal to see them. Other frogs stop moving and freeze like a statue when they see an enemy like a snake approaching — they are no doubt hoping not to be noticed. Many frogs hide away during the day, coming out mainly at night when they will not be seen.

A frog's wet, slippery skin is difficult to grasp, and this sometimes saves it from the jaws of its enemies. Some frogs produce poisons from special *glands* in the skin. They taste nasty and this makes predators spit them out of their mouths quickly. Many brightly colored frogs are extremely poisonous. Unlike other frogs, they have no need to hide away from their enemies — in fact, their colors act as a warning to predators that they taste unpleasant and may even cause death.

Grass snakes eat a lot of frogs. They hunt them both on land and in water.

This young dragonfly "nymph" has caught a tadpole in its powerful jaws.

Tadpoles and their enemies

Tadpoles have many enemies in a pond. They are an important food supply for many pond animals and are eaten in large numbers by water birds, fishes, newts, leeches, water-spiders, and by many insects and their larvae, including water-beetles, dragonflies, and water-bugs. Tadpoles are also eaten by frogs, even by their own parents, who may snap them up without realizing that they are killing their own offspring.

Snakes sometimes steal into the water to catch tadpoles.

A Three-spined Stickleback about to pounce on a young tadpole.

Very few of the large masses of young tadpoles manage to survive to become frogs. That is why the adults produce such enormous numbers of eggs — to make sure that at least one or two will live.

Tadpoles have very few ways of defending themselves compared to adult frogs. They are not so well camouflaged, especially when they are small and dark; in fact, they are all too easy to see as they wriggle about in the shallow water. As they grow bigger, their colors blend in better with their surroundings. They hide under stones and among water weeds for protection, especially during the day. At night they feed and move about more actively when they cannot be seen. They use their sense of smell to find food.

Tadpoles usually have no parents around to protect them, since most frogs leave their eggs and young to develop on their own. However, one exception is the Common Bullfrog: the male stays at the pond to guard the eggs and later to protect the young tadpoles from hungry predators. When tropical frogs guard their eggs and young, it is often the father which carries out this duty.

Some ponds get spoiled because people throw all kinds of rubbish into them.

Frogs and humans

Human beings unfortunately do a lot of harm to frogs. In many countries they are killed and eaten in large numbers; people especially enjoy eating frogs' legs, which are considered tender and delicious.

Frogs are also collected and killed for use in schools and colleges to help people learn about biology. Many are used in scientific experiments for medical research.

Other wild places are destroyed when the land is cleared to make way for roads or buildings.

Frogs are sometimes squashed by traffic on the roads when they are making their way to the breeding pools in spring. But the worst harm is done when people damage the wild places in which frogs live. Many frogs have died because their habitat has been spoiled or destroyed by human beings. Farmers drain their land to grow crops, and many ponds are bulldozed or covered over to make way for new buildings or roads. People throw all sorts of rubbish into ponds, and sometimes the water gets *polluted* by poisonous chemicals, such as weedkillers and *pesticides*, which are sprayed onto the land and then washed by rain into the streams which run into ponds.

Hundreds of ponds and other wet, marshy places are destroyed by people every year, and frogs are now much rarer than they used to be. Fortunately, many people are beginning to realize how important it is to save some of these wet places and to build new ponds wherever they can, so that frogs and other water-loving creatures can survive.

Taking large amounts of frogspawn or tadpoles out of a wild pond is harmful, too. If you want to collect some frogspawn to take home and study, take only a very small amount. Look after it carefully and return the young frogs to the same pond as soon as they have grown their legs and are ready to hop away.

This girl is looking at some frogspawn in a pond. She picks it up gently in her hands.

Newts are often found in ponds. This is a male Great Crested Newt.

Friends and neighbors

Frogs in a pond share their home with many other animals. Their close relatives, the toads, which usually spend a lot of time on land, always return to ponds to lay their eggs in the water. So do newts and salamanders, which are also amphibians. The eggs of all these animals hatch into young or larval forms, just like tadpoles, and these grow and develop into adults in a similar way.

However, these eggs are not all laid at the same time or in the same place. Frogs usually breed earlier in the year than toads and newts, and many tadpoles are well on the way to becoming frogs at the time when toads and newts are only just laying their eggs. Toads also lay their eggs in deeper water than frogs do. The long strings of toadspawn are wrapped around water weeds, while newts attach their eggs, singly, to the leaves and stems of various water plants.

Even so, these animals are often present together in one pond, and there is great competition for food and shelter. Many tadpoles are eaten by toads and newts, as well as by other frogs, and young newts are also eaten by adult frogs and toads.

Other animals living in a pond include snails, worms, beetles, and various kinds of insect larvae, many of which provide food for frogs. Frogs themselves have to beware of fishes and water birds, which are always on the look-out for a tasty meal.

Plants are another important part of the frog's habitat. A pond could not survive without its plants, because these give out oxygen into the water, and this helps to keep the animals alive. Water plants are also used as food by young tadpoles, and they provide a vital place of shelter for both young and adult frogs.

A Common European Toad. Toads, like frogs, return to ponds to lay their eggs.

Life in the pond

The lives of frogs and tadpoles are closely linked to the lives of many other animals and plants living in and around a pond. This is mainly because of what they eat. We can see this more clearly by drawing a diagram to show which animals eat what. As you can see, not only are frogs and tadpoles eaten by many other animals, but they themselves feed on a variety of smaller animals, which in turn have to find their food from even smaller animals or plants. Frogs and tadpoles are just one link in many of the food chains in which food and energy is passed from tiny plants and animals to larger predators such as fishes, snakes, and birds.

Food Chain

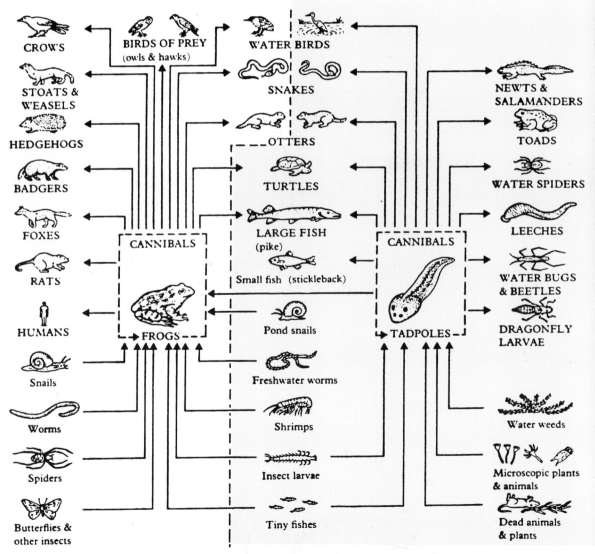

CROWS

BIRDS OF PREY
(owls & hawks)

WATER BIRDS

NEWTS &
SALAMANDERS

STOATS &
WEASELS

SNAKES

HEDGEHOGS

OTTERS

TOADS

BADGERS

TURTLES

WATER SPIDERS

FOXES

CANNIBALS

LARGE FISH
(pike)

CANNIBALS

LEECHES

RATS

Small fish (stickleback)

WATER BUGS
& BEETLES

HUMANS

FROGS

Pond snails

TADPOLES

DRAGONFLY
LARVAE

Snails

Freshwater worms

Worms

Shrimps

Water weeds

Spiders

Insect larvae

Microscopic plants
& animals

Butterflies &
other insects

Tiny fishes

Dead animals
& plants

This frog is very much at home as it sits half-in and half-out of the water.

Frogs are well suited to their life both in and around water. A pond is an ideal home for them. It is the place where they are born and the place to which they must return to lay their eggs. It provides many frogs with food and shelter, and it is also the nursery for their young, the place where their tadpoles feed and grow.

However, there are many dangers in such a small habitat, and the tadpoles have very little chance to escape, even though the adults can often hop away to safety. Fortunately, frogs produce so many offspring, that one or two usually manage to survive and carry on breeding.

But frogs can only survive if there are wet places for them to live. Human beings can help by protecting these habitats in the wild and by making new ponds. Most frogs can live quite happily in and around a pond. They will be fun to watch and may even help to keep down the insect pests around the pond.

Human beings can help frogs to survive by preserving wet places and building new ponds, like this one.

Glossary and Index

These new words about frogs appear in the text on the pages shown after each definition. Each new word first appears in the text in *italics*, just as it appears here.

amphibian .... an animal, such as a frog, toad, or newt, which lives both on land and in water. **2**

camouflage .. animal disguise — the way in which an animal hides by blending with its background so that it cannot easily be seen. **2, 6, 7, 8, 25**

cannibal .... an animal that eats its own kind. **13**

gills .... special branched structures, well supplied with blood, for breathing underwater. **17, 18**

glands .... parts of the body which produce a special substance, such as sweat, milk, or poison. **23**

habitat .... the natural home of any plant or animal. **3, 27, 29, 31**

hibernation .. period of sleep over winter. During hibernation, the body slows down, the heart rate drops, and the animal survives on its stored fat. **4, 14, 19**

larvae .... (plural of *larva*) the young that hatch from the eggs of insects and many water animals. **13, 28, 29**

membrane .... a thin layer of skin or tissue that covers or connects parts of an animal or plant. **8**

omnivorous .. feeding on many kinds of food, both animals and plants. **18**

pesticides ..... poisonous chemicals used to kill pests, especially insects. **27**

polluted .... made dirty and, therefore, spoiled or damaged. **27**

predators ..... animals that kill and eat other animals. **2, 8, 16, 23, 25, 30**

prey .... an animal that is hunted and killed by another animal for food. **12, 13, 22**

sperm .... (short for *spermatozoa*) male sex cells. **15**

Reading level analysis: SPACHE 4, FRY 7, FLESCH 74 (fairly easy), RAYGOR 6, FOG 7.5, SMOG 4.8

Library of Congress Cataloging-in-Publication Data

Coldrey, Jennifer.
  The frog in the pond.

  (Animal habitats)
  Summary: Describes, in text and photographs, the lives of frogs in their natural habitat explaining how they feed, defend themselves, and breed.
  1. Frogs—Juvenile literature. [1. Frogs] I. Oxford Scientific Films. II. Title. III. Series.
QL668.E2C776   1986   597.8   85-30300
ISBN 1-55532-084-8
ISBN 1-55532-059-7 (lib. bdg.)

North American edition first published in 1986 by Gareth Stevens Children's Books, 1555 North RiverCenter Drive, Suite 201, Milwaukee, Wisconsin 53212, USA. Text copyright © 1986 by Oxford Scientific Films. All rights reserved. No part of this book may be reproduced in any form or by any means without permission in writing from the publisher. Conceived, designed, and produced by Belitha Press Ltd., London. Series Editor: Jennifer Coldrey. U.S. Editors: MaryLee Knowlton & Mark J. Sachner. Design: Treld Bicknell. Line Drawings: Lorna Turpin. Scientific Consultants: Gwynne Vevers and David Saintsing.

The publishers wish to thank the following for permission to reproduce copyrighted material: **Oxford Scientific Films Ltd.** for pp. 1, 4 left, 25, 27, and 31 below (photographer David Thompson); pp. 2, 9 below, 14 above and below, 16, 17 above and below, 18 above left and right, below left and right, 19 left and right, 21 above, 22 above, 24 above, 26 above, and 28 (photographer G. I. Bernard); pp. 3 above, 9 above, and 26 below (photographer G. H. Thompson); p. 3 below (photographer John Paling); pp. 6 below, 7, 12 above and below, 15, 23, and 31 above (photographer Avril Ramage); pp. 4 right, 21 below, 24 below, and 29 (photographer J. A. L. Cooke); p. 5 (Mantis Wildlife Films); p. 6 above (photographer Jack Dermid); p. 8 (photographer Peter Parks); pp. 10 left and right and 11 (photographer Stephen Dalton); p. 13 (photographer M. P. L. Fogden); p. 20 (photographer G. H. Coe); and p. 22 below (photographer Stephen Mills). Front and back cover photographer: Avril Ramage.

Printed in the United States of America

3 4 5 6 7 8 9 96 95 94 93 92 91

For a free color catalog describing Gareth Stevens' list of high-quality children's books, call 1-800-341-3569 (USA) or 1-800-461-9120 (Canada).